THE LITTLE GUIDE TO

K-POP

Published in 2024 by OH!
An Imprint of Welbeck Non-Fiction Limited,
part of Welbeck Publishing Group.
Offices in: London – 20 Mortimer Street, London W1T 3JW
and Sydney – Level 17, 207 Kent St, Sydney NSW 2000 Australia
www.welbeckpublishing.com

ISBN 978-1-80069-575-7

Compiled and written by: Malcolm Croft
Editorial: Victoria Denne
Project manager: Russell Porter
Production: Marion Storz

A CIP catalogue record for this book is available from the British Library

Printed in China

10 9 8 7 6 5 4 3 2 1

THE LITTLE GUIDE TO

K-POP

사랑해

THE KOREAN MUSIC WAVE

OH!

CONTENTS

INTRODUCTION

As we slide further into the second decade of the 21st century, there is just one fact that we all know to be true: K-Pop rules the world. For more than 20 years since it first came to mainstream attention on Korean TV, pop music from South Korea was held at the border of its host nation, remaining a relatively local phenomenon, occasionally breaking free and allowing the world to see what dynamic dynamite lay hidden in that often overlooked part of the atlas.

Today, K-Pop is a global obsession where more than 80 million albums are sold each year and many tens of billions of streams, each one pioneering a path forward for all Asian music to be heard without prejudice on the world's airwaves, unlike ever before in music history. With its laser-precision dance acrobatics and razor-sharp choreography, infectious melodies and anthemic hooks and high-concept MVs – all driven by genuine inter-group chemistry by beautiful young people – K-Pop has everything a music fan could want all under one very dazzling umbrella.

Much like K-Pop blends together the genres of electronic, pop, hip-hop, rock and R&B, this tiny tome fuses together all the facts, stats, quotes and trivia you'll need to keep up to speed with this lightning bolt of an evolving genre. From BTS ("the Beatles of the YouTube Generation") to BLACKPINK, Seventeen to EXO, Red Velvet to SuperM, and every other idol in between, this compact compendium celebrates a global musical revolution in full swing and revels in the revelations of this unpoppable and unstoppable phenomenon. Enjoy!

CHAPTER
ONE

BIG BANG

And we're off! K-Pop has been an ever-inflating balloon for more than a decade straight and it has yet to burst. Let's dive deep into the belly of the beast from the East at the beginning and tell the story of K-Pop, one fandom, *maknae* and *hyung* at a time. Strap yourself in, it's going to be a wild ride…

대중음악

Daejungeumak

K-Pop in South Korea is obviously not called K-Pop. It is simply known formally as pop music, or *daejungeumak*.*

> * Younger, cooler Korean fans refer to K-POP more informally as *gayo*, or 가요, which translates simply as "song".

5%

The percentage of the 100 new groups that debut in South Korea every year that survive to find success.

K-Pop comes in generational waves:

First Generation – 1990–1999
(H.O.T.; S.E.S.; Fin.K.L)

Second Generation – 2000–2009
(g.o.d; TVXQ; Super Junior; BIGBANG)

Third Generation – 2010–2019
(BTS; EXO; Seventeen; BLACKPINK)

Fourth Generation – 2020–present
(ENHYPHEN; Stray Kids; ITZY; (G)I-dle)

K-Pop Idols #1: The Kim Sisters

The Kim Sisters are credited with inventing K-Pop and are considered the first South Korean music group to achieve success in the U.S. in the 1950s, with renditions of American pop songs sung completely phonetically; they appeared on the famous *Ed Sullivan Show* 22 times. Today, they are icons of Korean culture!

BILLION-VIEW CLUB

In December 2012, PSY's "Gangnam Style" – the first worldwide K-Pop hit – also became the first YouTube video to reach one billion views.

In May 2014, the song also became the first video to exceed two billion views. Go PSY!

A is for... aegyo!

Aegyo is when an idol group acts all cute. BTS's Jungkook is pure *aegyo*!

한국팝

K-Pop, in Hangul.

Fandoms #1

Each idol group's fandom has their own specially chosen name:

1. BTS – ARMY

2. BLACKPINK – BLINK

3. TXT – M.O.A (Moments of Alwaysness)

4. TWICE – ONCE

5. MONSTA X – Monbebe

6. Wonho – Wenee

7. SEVENTEEN – Carat (fans are valuable as diamonds!)

8. GOT7 – iGOT7

9. Red Velvet – ReVeluv

10. NCT – NCTzen

C is for... Comebacks!

Every year, K-Pop idol groups stage comebacks to support the release of new EPs, or trilogies, or new albums.

K-Pop Idols #2: Seo Taiji and Boys

Seo Taiji and Boys were the first-ever K-Pop group.

Leader Seo Taiji revolutionized Korean pop music when he merged it with popular American music and hip-hop choreography. Modern K-Pop was born!

"

H.O.T. expanded the spectrum of the K-Pop market. We didn't mean to set the trend. We had no choice but to grow the market by ourselves and did what we did best. The K-Pop market was born along the way.

"

Tony An, H.O.T., Yonhap News Agency, 2018

In 1885, an American missionary called Henry Appenzeller began teaching American and British folk songs at Korean schools. It was the first time Koreans had access to Western songs.

These songs were called *changga* in Korean and were often popular Western melodies, such as "Oh My Darling, Clementine", but with Korean lyrics.

K-Pop Idols #3: H.O.T.

H.O.T. (Highfive of Teenagers) are considered to be the first true K-Pop idol group because they were made up of trained pop stars. In 1997, they released the song "Candy" – and became the first superstar idol group of the first generation of K-Pop. They were founded by SM Entertainment's Lee Soo-man when he assembled five singers and dancers who represented what he believed Korean teens wanted to see from a modern pop group.

E is for...
Ending fairy!

An ending fairy is the member of a K-Pop group who gives a lingering look directly into the camera and makes a gesture, such as winking, at the end of a live or video performance.

The first ever pop song written by a Korean composer was "Nakhwayusu" ("Fallen Blossoms on Running Water") sung by Lee Jeong-suk in 1929.

It sounds nothing like modern K-Pop, but it was a start!

B is for... Bias!

Bias is the term for
a fan's favourite member
of their favourite K-Pop
idol group.

Hwaiting

A Korean expression a person might say to give themselves encouragement before a challenge or, if an idol, a big performance. Derived from the word "fighting".

F is for...
Fanchants!

Fanchants are catchphrases
that fans shout before an
idol's performance to show
their passion.

66

To the U.S. and the world,
I'm just known as some funny
song and some funny music,
some funny video guy.

99

PSY in 2012, the year that he took K-Pop global, thanks
to his breakout song, "Gangnam Style", followed by
"Gentleman" and "Hangover" – all three smashes!

7 years

The standard length of a K-Pop idol contract* with an entertainment agency. After this period, an idol is able to renegotiate better terms.

* A three-year contract for trainees must be completed first.

Shinhwa

This group are the longest continuously active group in the history of K-Pop – and are still going! Eric, Lee Min Woo, Kim Dong-wan, Shin Hye-sung, Jun Jin, and Andy formed the band in 1998. Aptly, Shinhwa means "legend", too, in English.

66

Our group name has a dual meaning. Black meaning strong and being confident and pink representing the feminine side of our group.

99

Jennie, BLACKPINK

G is for...
Gangnam!

Gangnam is a district in
Seoul, South Korea's capital,
known for its upmarket
shopping, dining, and hotels.
A place where idols, and the
wealthy, play.

K-Pop Idols #4: SuperM

In 2019, SuperM became the first K-Pop supergroup. The band features seven World Stars from four other internationally successful – and still active – K-Pop bands: EXO, WayV, NCT 127 and SHINee.

Ones to Watch: NewJeans

Five-member girl group NewJeans released their debut single, "Attention", in July 2022, and their debut EP got more than 1.9 million views on YouTube in one day. They also have more than 10 million monthly listeners on Spotify – so expect NewJeans to be your next favourite K-Pop band!

The first (and only!) Korean hip-hop band to be part of the initial Hallyu wave were called Drunken Tiger, formed in 1999.

Their debut album, *Year of the Tiger*, was so apart from the norm of conservative Korean pop culture that it became highly controversial. But like most pioneering artists, it quickly became lauded for its innovation and originality.

Top 10 K-Pop Bands in the World, 2023

Based on sales, socials and streams, these are the K-Pop bands still doing the biggest business…

1. BTS
2. BLACKPINK
3. EXO
4. NCT
5. Seventeen
6. ITZY
7. NewJeans
8. Stray Kids
9. TWICE
10. Red Velvet

H is for... Hyung!

Hyung in Korean means "older brother". All idol groups have a *hyung* that other members look up to.

K-Pop Idols #5: Rain

In 1998, Rain (Jung Ji Hoon) was the first K-Pop artist to find fame outside Korea. In 2007, Rain was even named *TIME* magazine's most influential person in the world, beating Beyoncé! He said at the time: "I would really like to see an Asian make it in the United States… and I would like that Asian to be me!" His dream came true.

Today, Rain remains one of the most famous South Korean singer-songwriters, producers and actors, starring in several Hollywood and Asian movies.

Founded in 1996 by Yang Hyun-suk, YG Entertainment – one of the big four in South Korea – does it all: record label, talent agency, music production company, event management and concert production company and even music publishing house. Many idols, and idol groups, have been created here, including Epik High, 1TYM, 2NE1, PSY, Big Bang, CL, Winner, iKon and BLACKPINK.

I is for... Idol!

A rookie transforms into an idol after a successful audition to become a member of an idol group. Very few make it this far.

66

It's clear that not only in Asia, but that many people from countries across the globe love K-Pop!

99

G-Dragon, on K-Pop, *Billboard*, February 21, 2013

자리바꿈

Jaribaggum

Jaribaggum is the famous synchronized formation changing in K-Pop where band members switch positions during a routine for maximum effect!

Can you name
the nine members
of **TWICE**?

Nayeon, Jeongyeon, Momo, Sana, Jihyo, Mina,
Dahyun, Chaeyoung and Tzuyu

"

In some places, we're the first K-pop group that can perform sell-out shows at U.S. arenas. It's an honour and, as a K-pop artist, I feel like another group can get some energy from us too. K-pop is not just GOT7; we're all family. GOT7, another group, different companies – we'll start right now and later we'll make K-pop bigger so another group can perform here too.

"

BamBam, Got7, on U.S. K-Pop success, *Billboard*, July 11, 2018

April 11, 1992

This is the day that K-Pop, as we know it now, was first performed live on South Korea's most-watched MBC TV talent show. K-Pop pioneers Seo Taiji and Boys performed "Nan Arayo" ("I Know") to an audience of bemused viewers.

They received the lowest rating from the jury – but a phenomenon was born!

사랑해

CHAPTER
TWO

HELLO HALLYU

K-Pop is the biggest slice of the *Hallyu* cake, for sure, and yes, of course, it's a red velvet cake. It's time now to learn as much as we can about this global mega phenomenon, so prepare your stomach – you're about to become stuffed on a whole lot of K-Pop culture…

178 million

The number of *Hallyu* fans now observed around the world in 2022, up from 9.26 million in 2012.

The first wave of *Hallyu*, the South Korean music and culture expansion westwards, was globally recognized in the 2000.

100 million

In 2009 – three years before PSY – Girls' Generation's song "Gee" became the first owners of a global K-Pop hit. In 2013, "Gee" became the first K-Pop song to reach 100 million views on YouTube.

Top K-Pop

According to *NME*, these are the top 10 K-pop tracks that defined 2023 (and we agree!):

1. "Queencard" – (G)I-DLE
2. "welcome to MY world" – aespa
3. "Cupid" – FIFTY FIFTY
4. "Attitude" – fromis_9
5. "I Am" – IVE
6. "Rover" – Kai
7. "ICKY" – KARD
8. "Eve, Psyche and the Bluebeard's Wife" – LE SSERAFIM
9. "Knock"– Lee Chaeyeon
10. "Honestly" – Limelight

포인트 안무

Pointeu anmu

PSY's "Gangnam Style", Super Junior's "Sorry Sorry" and BLACKPINK's "DDU DU DDU DU", are all examples of K-Pop's killer USP – point dancing, or *pointeu anmu*.

Point dancing movement is repetitive and addictive – purposely so to go viral – and perfectly matches the theme of the song.

"

The larger than life visuals allow fans who may not understand the language to still understand the music.

"

Scooter Braun, Justin Bieber and Ariana Grande's manager, on K-Pop visuals, BBC *Newsround*, July 12, 2019

On August 5, 2020, on the border between North and South Korea, three North Korean soldiers were caught listening and performing a dance to BTS's "Blood Sweat & Tears". They were dragged away, arrested and detained in a political prison camp, with the threat of execution.

North Korea's director of the Bureau of Security Affairs issued a propaganda statement that said the soldiers' "state of mind is completely rotten".

H is for... Hallyu!

Translation: the Korean wave.

Hallyu is the expansion of South Korean pop culture as a global cultural phenomenon, seen in everything from Korean dramas on Netflix to Korean food in Western restaurants. At the heart of *Hallyu* is K-Pop.

August 18–20

K-Con, the largest K-Pop convention in the world, has grown exponentially since its debut in 2012 in Los Angeles and is now held in more than 10 international locations. Idols and artists perform and fans find out about world stars of the future!

J is for...
Jeju Island!

Jeju Island is an exotic island paradise with crystal-clear water and golden sands – often described as the Hawaii of Korea. It also serves as the perfect set for dreamy K-dramas.

4,936,708,860,759

The amount of Korean Won
(₩) that BTS generates
per year for South Korea's
economy. It is the equivalent
of 3.9 billion U.S. dollars.

Anti-fans

K-Pop fans who target
less-liked band members
of particular idol groups
in an attempt to get them
disbanded or sink their
popularity.

D is for ... Delulu!

A delulu is a fan who believes that they have a chance of dating their favourite member of the band, or bias.

In 2006, TVXQ's U-Know Yunho was handed a bottle of orange juice from an anti-fan. The drink contained a poison and he soon began to feel sick. "It's a lie to say it got better quickly, but it got better gradually," Yunho said afterwards.

220 billion

The total amount of
K-Pop video views
on YouTube, as of
August 2023.

As of August 2023, these are the top ten K-Pop videos with more than one billion views on YouTube:

1. "Gangnam Style"*   PSY
2. "DDU-DU DDU-DU"   BLACKPINK
3. "Kill this Love"   BLACKPINK
4. "Dynamite"   BTS
5. "Boy with Luv"   BTS
6. "Boombayah"   BLACKPINK
7. "Gentleman"   PSY
8. "DNA"   BTS
9. "How You Like That"   BLACKPINK
10. "Mic Drop"   BTS

* 4.8 billion!

K is for... **Koreaboo!**

A non-Korean person obsessed with Korean popular culture.

Best Girl Groups

Now you know how to write your favourite girl groups in Hangul!

1. Twice – 트와이스
2. Red Velvet – 레드벨벳
3. (G)I-DLE – 아이들
4. MAMAMOO – 마마무
5. Momoland – 모모랜드
6. Girls' Generation – 소녀시대
7. Wonder Girls – 원더걸스
8. 2NE1 – 투애니원
9. T-ara – 티아라
10. Kara – 카라

Which K-Pop artist is known around the world as Mr Worldwide Handsome?

*Jin from BTS

L is for... Leader!

All K-Pop idol groups have a leader. They are the lead spokesperson and liaise between the group and their entertainment agency. BTS's leader is, of course, RM.

블랙핑크

BLACKPINK, in Hangul.

K-Pop Idols #6: BLACKPINK

BLACKPINK are the all-girl quartet that debuted in 2016 with the instant K-Pop classics "Boombayah" and "Whistle". They then found mega success with "DDU-DU DDU-DU" – the most-viewed music video by a K-Pop group on YouTube. Jennie, Rosé, Lisa and Jisoo were bought together as trainee idols by YG Entertainment, a Seoul-based talent agency and record label responsible for many other K-Pop acts, including K-Pop legend PSY.

With more than 100 songs recorded, BLACKPINK are the most prolific of all modern era K-Pop groups.

4.5 years

The average lifespan of a boyband K-Pop idol group. Girl groups is 3.3.

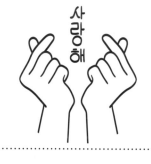

CHAPTER

THREE

GO
WEST

For decades, K-Pop has been slowly leaking out of the limits of its host nation.

Then, of course, in 2012, K-Pop exploded globally. Not only has K-Pop now broken the internet, it's also broken into and entered the homes of America, the hardest of all world music markets.

Let's look at the genre's journey from East to West, one titbit of trivia at a time…

66

We are still surprised that music created by South Korean artists reaches so many people around the world, transcending language and cultural barriers. We believe music is always an amazing and wonderful unifier of all things.

99

Jungkook, BTS, in a speech on anti-Asian hate crimes, White House, USA, May 31, 2022

S is for...
Sasaeng!

A *sasaeng* is an ultra-obsessive fan who stalks and invades the privacy of their favourite idol groups.

44.8%

In 2020, K-Pop had a record-breaking year to become the fastest-growth industry in the world –44.8 per cent!

Experts suggest the global pandemic was responsible for people in lockdown listening to new music.

2.1 billion

As of January 2023,
BLACKPINK's most viewed
song on their YouTube
channel was
"DDU-DU DDU-DU,"
since its release in
June 2018.

18

The average monthly amount spent, in U.S. dollars, on K-Pop music, in 2021.*

* K-Pop fans in the UAE spend the most per month – 27 U.S. dollars!

> **"**
> We are living in an
> era where the content
> industry resonates beyond
> geographical boundaries.
> K-Pop has become a
> global industry that can
> only continue to grow by
> targeting both domestic
> and international markets.
> **"**

Bang Si-Hyuk, HYBE founder and chairman, *Billboard*, February 1, 2023.

15.6 hours

The average monthly time spent listening to K-Pop music in 2023.

M is for... Maknae!

A word used to describe the youngest member of a K-Pop group.

South Korea's Military Service Act

All able-bodied men in South Korea are required to serve in the military for 18 months before they turn 28. Currently, only Olympic medalists and classical musicians are eligible for exemptions, K-Pop stars aren't, though that is expected to change imminently.

Suga, J-Hope and Jin are currently enlisted in the military until 2025. All BTS members enlistment should be complete by 2028.

66

You don't have to
understand Korean to
understand the music,
the visuals and the vibe.

99

Jisoo, BLACKPINK, *Billboard*, February 23, 2019.

66

We lived together for almost eight years before the debut, because we live in the same dorm and we are still living in the same dorm, so I think we are closer than family, our personal family, because we stay together, we sleep together, we eat together, we do everything together. We're getting old at the same time!

99

I.M., Monsta X, on their idol training, Consequence of Sound, December 3, 2021

U is for... Unnie!

In a K-Pop girl group, such as Red Velvet, an *unnie* is the oldest member in the group, or "big sister".

Sub-units

Many new groups, especially one with large member numbers, can sometimes form side projects, known as sub-units, working separately from the main group.

Perfect All-Kill (PAK)

This term is used to describe a K-Pop's all-round domination of the several Korean music charts on music streaming platforms, including iChart Weekly, Melon, Genie, Bugs, FLO, VIBE, and YouTube music.

BTS's track "Dynamite" was a perfect all-kill in 2020.

G-Dragon endured a total of 11 years of idol training before debuting with his now world-famous group, Big Bang.

"When I was a trainee I didn't stand out very much since I was only enthusiastic when it came to dancing. And I wouldn't consider myself good looking either. I could dance a bit but I wasn't a very good singer so I think it must've been difficult for the company [S.M.] to do anything with me at the time."

G-Dragon

N is for... **Nugu!**

Nugus are the idol groups that remain unknown or unsuccessful in the K-Pop industry. It means "a nobody".

> **"**
> I love BTS. I'm obsessed
> with watching the videos
> of them dancing.
> **"**

Shawn Mendes

66

I'm in the band. No, for serious. The security guard who tasered me was part of a carefully choreographed sequence me and the guys have been working on from our basement studio in my imagination.

99

Ryan Reynolds, K-Pop fan, about EXO, on Instagram, December 2, 2022

Ones to Watch: ENHYPEN

K-Pop boyband ENHYPEN formed in 2020, and the following year they released their debut album, *Border: Day One*. In 2022, they became the fastest K-Pop group to exceed one billion streams on Spotify. World domination is sure to follow.

K-Pop idols' diets are notoriously unhealthy.

In 2022, it was reported that several girl groups have a "Paper cup diet". This involves eating only nine paper cups' worth of food a day, with zero sugars or fats.

66

I've had to accept that – that everyone cannot love me. Because when there's love, there's hate. When there's light, there's dark. But it was really hard to accept as an artist that there's a lot of people that hate me, but on the other side, there are many more people who love me. I think everyone goes through that.

99

RM, BTS, on fame, Dazed and Confused, October 25, 2017

Bang Si-hyuk,
the man responsible for
BTS, founded the
entertainment agency Big
Hit, now HYBE, in 2005.

Major artists of theirs
include BTS, Seventeen,
TXT, LE SSERAFIM,
and NewJeans.
BTS bring in 85 per cent
of its revenue!

O is for... OMO!

The Korean version of OMG!

66

BLACKPINK in your area! When we say 'BLACKPINK in your area,' we're literally saying we're in your area with good music, with good energy – we're here for you.

99

Jennie, BLACKPINK, on their catchphase, *Elle*, September 17, 2020

66

Their song is stuck in my head the entire day. Like literally.

99

Camila Cabello, on TWICE's "Candy", IBTimes India, February 24, 2018

Killer K-Pop Choreography
The dance routines are just as
high energy and immaculate as
the songs – check them out!

1. "Gangnam Style" – PSY

2. "DNA" – BTS

3. "Bboom Bboom" – Momoland

4. "Bubble Pop" – Hyuna

5. "Mister" – Kara

6. "Ring Ding Dong" – SHINee

7. "Abracadabra" – Brown Eyed Girls

8. "Sorry Sorry" – Super Junior

9. "Gee" – Girls' Generation

10. "Coming of Age Ceremony" –
Park Ji-yoon

7.8 billion

The total number of #KpopTwitter tweets in 2021, up from 6.7 billion in 2020!

In June 2021, North Korean dictator Kim Jong-un called K-Pop a "vicious cancer" that was "corrupting young North Koreans' attire, hairstyles, speeches, behaviours".

He went on to say that if K-Pop continues to make its way into his heavily oppressed nation state, it would "make North Korea crumble like a damp wall". Time for change.

"

When we work for GOT7 we're seven individuals, who work in unison. We're a rainbow that offers seven different colours.

"

Jackson Wang, GOT7, on his group's bond, NYLON, August 6, 2018

"

It's difficult for me to say things like A led to B. But what I can say is that BTS' success in the U.S. market was achieved by a formula different from the American mainstream formula. Loyalty built through direct contact with fans had a lot to do with that.

"

Bang Si Hyuk, on BTS's success, *TIME* magazine, October 8, 2019

66

When we first debuted, there were 13 of us so it always took time to agree upon something. We've grown to understand each other as time passed, and came to learn how to take care of each other, rely on each other, and express our feelings. Our teamwork really developed further with time. That's why we never hesitate to show affection towards one another. We constantly try to encourage each other whenever, wherever we can.

99

Hoshi, Seventeen, on the group's affection for each other, *Teen Vogue*, August 2, 2022

K-Pop boyband Seventeen has 13 members. Their name is actually derived from the expression "13 members + 3 units + 1 group", which represents how the 13 members are divided into three different units and come together to form one awesome group. It's needlessly confusing – but fun!

So, can you name all 13 members of Seventeen?*

* S.Coups, Wonwoo, Mingyu, Vernon (the four of whom make up Seventeen's Hip-Hop Unit), Woozi, Jeonghan, Joshua, DK, Seungkwan (the five of whom make up the Vocal Unit), Hoshi, Jun, The8 and Dino (who make up the Performance Unit).

As of August 2023,
BLACKPINK member
Lisa is the most
followed K-Pop artist
on Instagram. That's the
entire population
of Vietnam!

"

When we were training, that system was very different, it wasn't set up properly so it wasn't that great of an environment. There's been a huge improvement since – companies have officially set up and are concerned about all-round things, including mental health.

"

Minhyuk, Monsta X, on the gruelling idol training and his mental health, *Rolling Stone*, January 25, 2022

사랑해

CHAPTER
FOUR

POP IDOLS

K-Pop comes in all shapes and sizes, and in all the colours of the rainbow. But it is today best known for its idol groups that are making and breaking waves on foreign shores.

There are hundreds to choose from, and lots to learn about who they are, and what they want from us, so we'd better get started…

In a 2022 global survey,
it was concluded
that K-Pop is popular
worldwide for its catchy
rhythm and choruses and
the attractiveness and
stylishness of its singers.

81%

The percentage of K-Pop fans who use YouTube to access South Korean pop music (K-Pop) content. Watching YouTube is the most common fan activity.

30.3 billion

The most viewed music channel on YouTube is the K-Pop group BLACKPINK – a Guinness World Record!

90.4 million!

As of September 2023, BLACKPINK have the highest number of subscribers of any K-Pop artist on YouTube.

800,000*

The number of yearly visitors who travel to South Korea – simply because of BTS – according to the Hyundai Research Institute.

* That's one in every 13 tourists!

66

I was immediately drawn to their fierce and empowering energy. They are not just giving you hit songs – they are sending a message that resonates beyond the lyrics.

99

Dua Lipa, on BLACKPINK, who collaborated with them on 2018's "Kiss and Make Up"

K-Pop Idols #7: Red Velvet

Irene, Seulgi, Wendy, Joy and Yeri made their debut for S.M. Entertainment in 2014, with the song "Happiness". Their high-energy live performances and killer high-concept MVs have earned them many ReVeluvs! They are also one of the first K-Pop groups to delve into "dual concept" musical releases. The "Red" half of their identity encourages bright and fun pop/disco songs (like singles "Ice Cream Cake", "Dumb Dumb" and "Red Flavor"), while the "Velvet" half allows them to explore their more mature and edgy side – "Bad Boy", for example.

S.M. Entertainment is South Korea's largest entertainment company.

Established in 1995 by Lee Soo-man, it led the way with K-Pop idol groups, including S.E.S., BoA, TVXQ!, Super Junior, Girls' Generation, SHINee, f(x), EXO, Red Velvet, NCT and H.O.T.

"

Through auditions, we discover hidden talent and put them through three to seven years of music, dance and acting training in order to create a star that's close to perfection. It's through this unique system that the Hallyu wave was created.

"

Lee Soo-man, founder of S.M. Entertainment, on Hallyu, *Allkpop*, June 13, 2011

"

The most difficult thing for me wasn't the physical training. It was the mental side of it and thinking, 'Will I ever make it?' Not knowing that is the most difficult part.

"

Jinhwan, iKON, on idol training, BBC *Newsround*, July 12, 2019

"

These days, we have no boundaries when it comes to work. Even on our days off, we're basically at the studio recording. Life is work, and work is life!

"

Jennie, BLACKPINK, on their work/life balance, *Elle*, September 17, 2020

"

I'd say fashion is like armour that makes me feel safe, protected, and confident. It's such a powerful medium for musicians when it comes to self-expression. Fashion and music go hand in hand and allows us to express our music visually, heightening the overall experience for the audience. I appreciate all different kinds of fashion and how it completes me as an artist and as a person.

"

Joy, Red Velvet, on the importance of fashion, *Vogue*, October 8, 2021

Ones to Watch: FIFTY FIFTY

On February 24, 2023, the four-member K-Pop group FIFTY FIFTY released their debut song, "Cupid", in both Korean and English. Overnight, the song became a viral TikTok sensation and made the girls the fastest K-Pop act to make it into *Billboard*'s Hot 100 chart. The song, as of August 2023, has 120 million views. It's a banger.

"

When we debuted, I was awkward seeing my face in pictures because there were lots of interviews and taking my photos and they'd script it and put it on the internet. That was so strange, I felt so strange. I didn't like my own face. Sometimes I might see some ugly pictures and be sad or be like 'oh shit' but that's OK because fans will see them. They even like our ugly faces, too. It doesn't matter.

"

I.M., Monsta X, on being perceived as an object by fans, *Rolling Stone*, January 25, 2022

> **"**
> When I was younger, I watched this four-member girl group called BESTie performing on TV and smiling brightly onstage. I absolutely fell for their performance and that inspired me to dream of becoming an artist and idol.
> **"**

Saena, FIFTY FIFTY,* on idol inspiration, *NME*, February 24, 2023

* The next HUGE K-Pop girl group

JJCC

In 2014, worldwide movie legend Jackie Chan, a life-long fan of K-Pop, formed his own idol group.

The name stands for "Jackie Chan Joins Cultures" and is pronounced Double-J-C, but can be translated as "Jackie Chan, let's spread K-Pop!" They haven't had much success – yet!

Sasaeng taxi

These special taxi services allow obsessive fans to follow their favorite K-Pop idols from location to location. They can cost more than $600 and will follow an idol or group for the entire day.

Biggest Boy Bands

If you've ever wanted to know the names
of your favourite boy band groups in
the Korean alphabet, now you do…

1. iKON – 아이콘

2. Seventeen – 세븐틴

3. GOT7 – 갓세븐

4. NCT – 엔시티

5. MONSTA X – 몬스타엑스

6. Stray Kids – 스트레이 키즈

7. Super Junior – 슈퍼주니어

8. SHINee – 샤이니

9. Big Bang – 빅뱅

10. 2PM – 투피엠

11. EXO – 엑소

12. TVXQ – 동방신기

"

The K-Pop fandom is very vocal.
They will make their opinions heard,
even if you don't put in much
effort to gauge what they want.
We wouldn't be doing our jobs if
we didn't take the time to listen.

"

Bang Si-Hyuk, on K-Pop, *Bollywood Life*,
September 5, 2019

66

We can just look one another in the eye and know immediately what we need to do for them and what we need to do for the team. Because we have this really special and strong teamwork, I think a lot of the fans are able to experience that positive energy. I hope we're able to give some positive impact to fans.

99

Jennie, BLACKPINK, on the band's strong bond, *Elle*, September 17, 2020

An entertainment agency's cost, according to the *Wall Street Journal*, of training a trainee to become an idol.

Jjang

In English this word translates as "the best". Really emphasize the "g" when pronouncing it. Which K-Pop band is your *jjang*?

Ulzzang

If you're the *ulzzang* in an idol group it means you have the "best face" and are considered the most good-looking member in the band. Any idols spring to mind?

44.4%

The percentage of K-Pop
idols who use stage names.

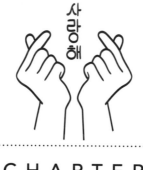

사랑해

CHAPTER
FIVE

DYNAMIC DYNAMITE

BTS are the undisputed champions of K-Pop. No other group has ever been as rapturously received (even though BLACKPINK are hot on their heels!).

Yes, BTS deserve a whole chapter all to themselves because, frankly, they're worth every word, as I'm sure you'll soon agree...

❝

This is your generation now.

❞

Seo Taiji, to BTS, on stage in Seoul, September 3, 2017

P is for... Pabo!

In K-Pop, a *pabo* is someone who acts stupid or foolish.

66

Our genre is just BTS. That debate between whether BTS is K-Pop or pop is very important for the music industry, but it doesn't mean very much for us members.

99

RM, BTS, on K-Pop, *Rolling Stone*, May 2021

"

K-Pop includes videos, clothes, choreography, social media. It is the total arts package.

"

RM, BTS, interview with Naomi Pike, *Vogue*, October 11, 2018

Bestselling K-Pop Albums in South Korea, 2011–2022

1. 2011   "The Boys" – Girls' Generation
2. 2012   "Sexy, Free & Single" – Super Junior
3. 2013   "Growl" – EXO-K
4. 2014   "Overdose" – EXO-K
5. 2015   "EXODUS" – EXO-K
6. 2016   "Wings" – BTS
7. 2017   "Love Yourself: Her" – BTS
8. 2018   "Love Yourself: Answer" – BTS
9. 2019   "Map of the Soul: Persona" – BTS
10. 2020   "Map of the Soul: 7" – BTS
11. 2021   "Butter" – BTS
12. 2022   "Proof" – BTS

7.5 trillion
South Korean won

BTS's HYBE agency has the highest market value on the South Korean stock exchange market, and is worth the equivalent of $5 billion U.S. dollars. Wow!

1.8 billion

As of August 2023, BTS's most viewed song on YouTube is "Dynamite", since its release in August 2020.

4,943%

The percentage increase in record sales of BTS's agency, HYBE, from 2016 to 2022, or 1.8 trillion South Korean won ($1.3 billion U.S. dollars).

In 2022, **BTS** was the top-selling K-Pop artist in South Korea with 12.4 per cent of total album sales, followed by **Stray Kids**, **Seventeen**, and **NCT DREAM**.

BTS was the best-selling K-Pop artist of 2023 with 34 million album sales, followed by **NCT** (24 million) and **EXO** (14 million).

"

The seven of us went towards a united goal with all we've got. I want BTS to go on for a long time, but for that to happen I think I have to retain who I am. What I know for sure is that we're BTS, and we made it here thanks to you. I always want to be RM of BTS. And I always want the future to be in front of us.

"

RM, BTS, on the future of BTS, *The Guardian*, June 15, 2022

Adorable
Representative
M.C.
for
Youth

BTS's fandom, the ARMY, is actually
an acronym, as well as a noun.

2 billion

The number of online mentions of BTS in the 10 years they have been world-famous, an average of 550,000 mentions every single day.

BTS hold more than 25 Guinness World Record titles, including:

The fastest to reach 1 million followers on Instagram (just 43 minutes!)

Most followed music group on Instagram

Most followed music group on TikTok

Most followed music act on Twitter

Most streamed group on Spotify

Most tickets sold for a livestreamed concert

66

We are not exceptional people – our plate is small. We're these rice-bowl-size guys getting so much poured into it. It's overflowing.

99

Suga, BTS, being humble, *Billboard*, August 26, 2021

R is for... Rookie!

K-Pop groups under two years old don't have idols as members, they have Rookies. Some groups, such as BLACKPINK, BTS or NCT, who have big success in their first two years, are known as Monster Rookies!

K-Pop Idols #8: BTS

BTS was first formed in 2013 by Big Hit Entertainment, now known as HYBE. They are, of course, the most popular K-Pop group in the world, thanks to their fans and fandom known as the "ARMY".

From oldest to youngest, the band's seven members are Jin, Suga, Rap Monster or RM (the group's leader), J-Hope, Jimin, J-Hope, V and Jungkook, the maknae.

66

The seven of us have pushed each other to be the best we can be. It has made us as close as brothers.

99

RM, BTS, *TIME* magazine, interview with Raisa Bruner, June 28, 2017

Saranghae

An informal way of idols saying
"I love you" in Korean to fans.

66

The road up to here has been arduous. It's taken a toll on my health, and I think we've put in every bit of our youth and more.

99

Jungkook, BTS, on their gruelling work schedules, *Billboard*, August 26, 2021

Before Jin broke away from BTS for his mandatory military enlistment in 2022, one of the first of the group to do so, Jin teamed up with Chris Martin of Coldplay to release one final song, a dedication of love to BTS's ARMY for all their support. The song is called "The Astronaut".

66

I don't think we could ever
be part of the mainstream
in the U.S., and I don't want
that either. Our ultimate
goal is to do a massive
stadium tour there. That's it.

99

RM, BTS, on American success, *Billboard*,
August 26, 2021

"

I actually wrote a song that I hear BTS might be messing with. It's the first K-Pop song I've had the honour of helping write. I really like BTS, I think they're great!

"

Ed Sheeran, on "Make It Right", *Billboard*, November 20, 2018

66

One of our producers, Pdogg, brought RM's demo tape to me and said, 'This is what the young kids are into.' RM was 15 at the time. I signed him immediately. I had considered putting together a hip-hop crew, not an idol group. But when I considered the business context, I thought a K-Pop idol model made more sense. Because many trainees wanted to pursue hip-hop and didn't want to be in an idol band, they left. At that time RM, Suga, and J-Hope stayed back, and they remain BTS's musical pillars. From there, through auditions, we discovered and added members that had more of an idol-like quality to the group.

99

Bang Si-Hyuk, on BTS's formation, *TIME* magazine, October 8, 2019

One in three K-Pop music sales and streams in the U.S. is BTS.

66

When we were 20, we had the guts. We charged forward without looking. Now we're more prudent. I've become calmer. There are more things to consider in my head.

99

Jimin, BTS, on ten years at the top, *Billboard*, August 26, 2021

> **"**
> BTS had some struggles in their earlier years. But I hoped they could become a group that was bigger than One Direction in their prime.
> **"**

Bang Si-Hyuk, on K-Pop, *Bollywood Life*, September 5, 2019

T is for... Trainees!

Before rookies become idols, they must first be trainees.

The training of idols, often as young as 10 years old, is an exhausting and disciplined process and can take more than five years before idolization occurs.

16 of the
50 most liked tweets
ever are by BTS.

BTS's fandom, the ARMY, the largest fanbase in K-Pop, is estimated to contain around 80 million fans.

Or, put another way, the entire population of Germany!

BTS are secretly popular in North Korea. To hide the fact from the North Korean military, fans use the code word of "Bangtan Bag" for the band. Specialized military units are trained to detect and persecute K-Pop fans north of the DMZ.

The North Korean government believes K-Pop is South Korean propaganda that could influence North Korean citizens to rise up against the nation's cruel dictator, Kim Jong-un.

In 2017, BTS officially changed the meaning of their acronymic name from Bangtan Sonyeondan, or Bulletproof Boy Scouts, to Beyond The Scene.

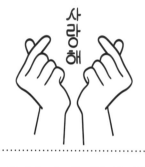

CHAPTER
SIX

GEE WHIZZ

It's time to do what K-Pop groups do best before the house lights come on and everyone leaves the building exhausted – hit the fans with a melodic medley of all the greatest hits everybody wants to sing along to.

These are the classic facts, secrets and ingredients that everybody needs to know about K-Pop…

Top Ten K-Pop Playlist

According to *Rolling Stone* magazine, these are the top 10 songs that define the K-Pop genre:

1. "Gee" – Girls' Generation
2. "Candy" – H.O.T.
3. "Good Day" – IU
4. "Spring Day" – BTS
5. "Short Hair" – Cho Yong Pil
6. "DDU-DU DDU-DU" – BLACKPINK
7. "Haru Haru" – BIGBANG
8. "I am the best" – 2NE1
9. "I Know" – Seo Taijii and Boys
10. "Tell Me" – Wonder Girls

Fandoms #2

1. 2NE1 – BlackJack
2. (G)I-DLE – Neverland
3. Big Bang – VIP
4. Evol – Voller
5. EXO – EXO-L
6. Girls' Generation – SONE
7. H.O.T. – Club HOT
8. Itzy – Midzy
9. iKON – iKONIC
10. Mamamoo – MooMoo

"

It's very surprising to us. All the records are the results of our fans, BLINKs, and their unconditional support. Every day we try to acknowledge how grateful we are, but more than the pressure, we are ready to give them back as much as they gave us. It just gives us more motivation to go further than we ever dreamed of.

"

Jennie, BLACKPINK, on their success, Grammy.com, September 2020

"

When I was training, I was walking a dark tunnel and you don't know when that is going to end. You don't know how you're going to make the debut or how you're gonna be on stage. I don't even know if I'm gonna get kept by the company or not so you get so anxious and there's lots of pressure. I only relaxed when I debuted.

"

I.M., Monsta X, on the pressures of training and debut, *Rolling Stone*, January 25, 2022

66

We've got so much Korean culture and so much Western culture in us.

99

Rosé, BLACKPINK, *Billboard*, February 23, 2019

"

On an overseas tour, I was really moved by our international fans who memorized the lyrics in Korean and sang along to all our songs. They even made a special chant for each song. It blew my mind in the best way possible!

"

Joy, Red Velvet, on English fans singing in Korean, *Billboard*, August 23, 2021

Selca

Korean for "selfie",
a popular way for idols
to engage with fans on
Instagram.

"

Music doesn't always originate from the UK or the States. It's global, it's Asia, it's the most random places you can imagine. I'm very proud that we all originated from different parts of the world.

"

Rosé, BLACKPINK, on their heritage, *Elle*, September 17, 2020

K-Pop Idols #8: Girls' Generation

In South Korea, Girls' Generation are the "Nation's Girl Group". In 2017, *Billboard* labelled them the "Top K-Pop Girl Group of the Past Decade". The group has eight members: Taeyeon, Sunny, Tiffany, Hyoyeon, Yuri, Sooyoung, Yoona and Seohyun.

66

Rosé, Jennie, Jisoo and Lisa are going to set the standard for the new girl group in America. We haven't had anyone like them since Destiny's Child. BLACKPINK is going to fill that void.

99

Bekuh Boom, on BLACKPINK, *Elle*, September 17, 2020

> **"**
> Somebody comes in
> with a piece of paper
> and stick it on a wall,
> and it would say who
> did best, who did worst,
> and who's going home.
> **"**

Jennie, Blackpink, on their idol training, *Elle*, September 17, 2020

Top 10 K-Pop Collabs

"Sour Candy" – BLACKPINK and Lady Gaga

"My Universe" – BTS and Coldplay

"Physical" – Hwasa and Dua Lipa

"Butter" – BTS and Megan Thee Stallion

"Written in the Stars" – Wendy and John Legend

"Nrilia" – G-Dragon and Missy Elliott

"Hangover" – PSY and Snoop Dogg

"Left and Right" – Jungkook and Charlie Puth

"Walking" – Jackson Wang and Joji

"Lo Siento" – Super Junior, Leslie Grace and Play-N-Skillz

Right now,
there are more than
300
K-Pop bands in
the world!

1,400

The number of trainees currently in South Korea preparing to be the next idol and world star!

6 out of 10

The ratio, according to
Statista, of the average
debut rate of trainees.
The rest go home.

The album *FML* by Seventeen, released in April 2023*, is the best-selling album of all time in South Korea, with more than 6 million copies sold.

* Before Seventeen, Kim Gun-mo's 1995 album *Wrongful Meeting* had been the best-selling South Korean album for 24 years!

K-Pop Idols #9: Super Junior

Debuting in 2005, Super Junior once held the honour of being the bestselling K-Pop group four years in a row. The group became famous for their highly acrobatic and high-energy choreography, as well as anthemic, addictive songs, such as "Sorry Sorry". Their fans are called E.L.F's – Ever Lasting Friends! They are still active.

W is for... World Star!

Any K-Pop idol who becomes a celebrity in South Korea or internationally.

66

When we first debuted, this word 'K-Pop', it wasn't such a big phenomenon as it is now. But when we started to get really popular with "Sorry Sorry", K-Pop as a whole became such a huge sensation. We want to continue to grow as a group, so that when the public thinks 'K-Pop', Super Junior becomes a household name that is very much relevant to 'K-Pop'.

99

Leetuk, Super Junior, on K-Pop, *Billboard*, June 27, 2018

JYP Entertainment is the second largest entertainment company in South Korea. Founded by Park Jin-young in 1997, JYP has transformed the lives of many trainees including GOT7, TWICE, Stray Kids, Itzy, Rain, g.o.d and Wonder Girls.

Y is for... Yeobo!

A Korean term of endearment used between Korean couples, translated as "sweetie", or "dear".

"

I can't believe it's been seven years already! Time flies when you're having fun and doing something that you love. ReVeluvs have kept us strong during the last seven years as we tried different concepts both visually and musically. That being said, I'd like to take this opportunity to say thank you for all your love and support! It means the world to us, and we'll continue to try our best to bring great music, performances, and fashion to you guys. Thank you, and we love you!

"

Wendy, Red Velvet, on their success, *Vogue*, October 8, 2021

1.62 trillion

The decrease, in sales revenue, in South Korean won ($1.2 billion U.S. dollars), that HYBE expects with the "extended break" of BTS. All other K-Pop entertainment companies are forecast to experience super growth.